WORDS ON EDGE

Michael Leong

BSE

ISBN: 978-0-9898103-9-5

BSE Books are distributed by
  Small Press Distribution
  1341 Seventh Street
  Berkeley, CA 94710
  orders@spdbooks.org | www.spdbooks.org | 1-800-869-7553
BSE Books can also be purchased at www.blacksquareeditions.org
and www.hyperallergic.com

Contributions to BSE can be made to
  Off the Park Press, Inc.
  972 Sunset Ridge
  Bridgewater, NJ 08807
(Please make checks payable to Off the Park Press, Inc.)

To contact the Press please write:
  Black Square Editions
  1200 Broadway, Suite 3C
  New York, NY 10001

An independent subsidary of Off the Park Press, Inc. Member of CLMP.
Publisher: John Yau
Editors: Ronna Lebo and Boni Joi
Design & composition: Shanna Compton

Cover image: Gary Stephan, "The Future of Reading 1," 2016, acrylic on canvas, 40″X 30″,
garystephanstudio.com. Courtesy of the artist.

CONTENTS

Politics and the English Language

Ignition Compendium

Word of the year 2016: for Merriam-Webster, 'surreal' trumps
'fascism.' —www.theguardian.com, 19 December 2016

To wake late in the not-too-distant 20th Century
to the fragrance of the digital future
on fire . . .

        It started with the lifelong quest
    of the ancients to pass judgement
    on the abstract use
    of music and voting machines.

They who perished in the name of long-term contradiction
say "cinema"
will not be the word of the year.

      La palabra en inglés is "anonymous."

La lupita says that the evening star will arrive thrashing over the church spire, and the so-
called "Drain Event" will bring an enigmatic, almost 1930s, resonance into the street.

Now
you are browsing
the weird infrastructure   of yesterday's dreams—

    to shave black ice
      from subway rails,

     to rescue the single lumen
  that's been knocking
  on the door from inside
  the dark archive.

     What emerges
has come to undo

the nails of recreational fascism,
riling children to tag the wall
with pragmatic blues, with a new
and creepy end to
Revolutionary Tangent #5.

EU-style expert warns rear view victory
could legitimize luxury
after tragedy.
         A flummadiddle
of southern spice and discontent
echoes the narrative drum loop of capitalism.

    (VIDEO):

    My-Little-Pony Empire trumps
    Trump-style security conference.

    (VIDEO):

    "Unstoppable" F-35 Stealth Fighter
    trampled by Harajuku-style puppy.

In his online address, Trump was announcing
four more years of a year-round coup
against Death Star's dystopia.

        "We are going to build
        that politically bigly brothel
        and make the academic
        anarchists pay for it."

    Moving into view,
the large and menacing turkey head

started to feed on what was left
of the white, saccharine mush
of America.

Caught between his slapstick,
tech-altered hat and his intractable,
"trickle-down" toupée,

    the corpse of November
continues protesting.

Politics and the English Language
(George Orwell Through the Looking Glass)

So the poet who speaks with the fire of alchemical fervor, stuns and
deflates the nexus of Orwellian tumours . . . —Will Alexander

A not unblack dog was chasing a not unsmall rabbit
across a not ungreen field. Then the field folded and flowered;
then the field became, in fact, not green.

"*No!*" said the not unsmall rabbit to the not unblack dog
and the dog, now covered in *forget-me-nots*, went along
on his merry, forgetful way.

"*No!*" said the not unsmall rabbit to the not green field,
and a miniature not ungreen stage
miraculously sprang out of the *snapdragons*.

Then the not unsmall rabbit hopped onto the tiny,
not ungreen proscenium, cleared his throat,
and said,
      "I returned and saw under the sun,
these images clash, infused
by their own virtual reflection:

        a white canker on a black stone,
        an iron bugle thinking in numbers,
        a plastic dove spurting out ink.

I do not want to exaggerate.

Defenseless villages are bombarded from the air.
I habitually see a huge, concrete swan
rising out of poisoned waters.

There is war between English ducks
and Russian cuttlefish, between Catholic cavalry horses

and Italian Operators masquerading
as the German petty-bourgeoisie, between the alien voice
of Japan and the subaqueous Latin machine.

Meanwhile, the Saxon dog and its international sect
have disappeared underneath the white lion's
nationalist chariot.
                              In Arctic lumber camps,
Professor Hyena is defending millions of communist maidens
now with Shakespeare's electric trident,
now with Mr. X's Whitmanesque cudgel of nonsense, now with
Achilles' transparent buckler and sword.

The struggle was like bombs of neurotic jargon
dropping on a prefabricated henhouse—
like a language in which *eyes*
means *bullseyes*, in which
frivolous bread is translated out of existence.

So much for atmospheric democracy at nine o'clock.

One cannot change all this schizophrenia in a moment,
just as one need not swallow
a seventeenth-century sphere full of mirrors and light.
For in real life it is always
the anvil that tricks the hammer by visualizing
unfashionable noises braying
against the bloodstained, incendiary air.

It is clear that few journalists explore the false limbs
of a midsummer *cul de sac*
or the historic discs that indefinitely
cut across the long passages of time,
but, at any rate, us undersecretaries should begin

the invasion of the dustbin
and mend our homemade banner tacked together
from living candles, random
tea leaves, medieval spectacles, twisted bullets
that can image the future, and silly
manifestos found in a countryside dump.
If one fails amply enough, such variations
of bittersweet sound can change the atom
and its trembling desires, or at least
recognize the sadness of order in a packet of chaos.

The point is that the process is reversible.
Go test the Lancelot hypothesis.
Put your ears to the gap when the light catches your larynx.
Ask, if you must, the unconscious stenographer
gumming together long strips of words on the haunted
frontiers of consciousness.

We have to take hansom cabs along imaginary roads
to find, inadvertently, outcrops of the real:
an anticlimax to some, but to others,
a dialect on the other side of *etc.*
infinitely rushing through the tide of the present.

One's brain is, therefore, like an octopus—
emotional, bashful, and sometimes clear.

So I end by dictating to you, the reader,
some irreducible if question-begging questions:
'Have I said anything that is avoidably ugly?
What words will express it
against the inexorable *Weltanschauung*,
the thorny syntax of the wind?

Could I tabulate it in a foreign pamphlet,
in some melting,
                    non-fragmentary dream?'

In our time,
            is the dictionary not a cannibal?"

the transmission of (other subsurface agents may be considered necessary for underground Control

for E. J. McAdams

at the end of The geothermal Paragraph
exploration of the fluid field

Square-shaped forms had amassed mysteriously
in the air while the jagged, ad hoc equation
became like a silent backdrop, occasionally seeping
into the already tainted central-nervous-system of the town.
The people were used to being ensconced in their own
pressurized shadows, to perusing newspapers for headlines
like "Designer Vanity in the Abscessed Administration" or
"Science Concludes That the Earth Is Patriotic" or
"How to Get Rid of Hydraulic Vice."
                              While millions of dollars
were being dispersed in the hemorrhaging greenhouse,
they wondered, "Why are the limits not off limits, too?"

Landowners ground their teeth,
their children desperately lobbying to move those who
would suspend the law in formaldehyde
to place public pumps and systems into the deep basin of suffering.

There were some who called for a firsthand data splicer
to open up the arteries of misrepresentation
and remediate the idiopathic word. They made a sign
towering high above the derricks and tarp-lined pits
that said, "The horses of lack are grander than the cows of revenue."

They filed away high levels of volatile soil
into the worthless
but resource-intensive record, turning a conventional formation
into an unnatural seepage of cloud. It spread around the county,
carving a renewable story without a center.

In a written statement to the press, the Department of Permissible Dizziness
provided a sampled comment—

"A detailed review of our operations reveals
a slick frontier where the surface of the environment
is intermingling with another governing surface.
We disclosed a natural mist to see the trouble between source and resource
and have taken the controversial drop in the bucket off the table.
The liquefied transition scarred early and ultimately became murky
but there is already the possibility of fully processing
the logical issues in clear and technological terms."

According to oil-and-gas executives, no one really knows
the difference between the film *Gasland* and *2012*,
so they say there's nothing to be afraid of,
but a newly constructed awareness is now imagining us,
is drinking our proprietary information as we speak.
To identify it would be like injecting millions
of gallons of uncertainty into the expected precipitate
or making a poorly understood loophole in time.

A residual wave swoops down,
spills its domestic deposits, but refuses to die
as a fog traces unleased and free-flowing patterns
into the galvanized Earth.
Below the bridge which stretches
from the massive past to the dizzying present
the groundwater of pure possibility is rolling spontaneously
into the white beard of life.
Between the unknown and the known,
the power of a carbon-based form to imagine
can evaporate even absence—
as if klieg lights were installed and actually pointing
at the most radical repositories of non-disclosure.

When presence is bent, the shock of the real
showers entire landscapes
with a thin layer of unconventional communications,

making people colloquially believe that the local and global
are parallel as well as at an angle
since a mouth from the open-air moratorium is now speaking.

It says the volatile *now* must be accessed via the unfiltered future.
It says fire is spreading throughout the infrastructure of water.
It says here is evidence belonging to a bleeding machine.
It says the evacuated position no longer stands.

The slow rush of the finite gradually blew up
like some satellite full of cracks
sweeping accidental materials into the vertical silt.

What was understood to be a collateral planet behind the horizon
turned out to be just a bubble, as seen
through the insidious
scope of industry. The federal degradation provider
declined to comment.

Above the pristine, tree-covered hedge fund,
a time compressor
that turned millions of centuries into just one or two years
mysteriously combusted,
contaminating even the vast mutagens of decades to come.

In a city west of innovation, figures in hazmat suits
found mysterious maps without the framework of a central atlas
and an animated transistor board trying to will a visible message
in the strata of light.

A huge black hand of smoke was writing a gaseous testimony
across the burned and clicking album of the ground.

Meanwhile, trapped within the closed-door compounds of Progress,
researchers had lodged thousands of complaints
against their computers which, though offline, went on typing:

> *boom, fracking, fracking, fracking,*
> *fracking, fracking, fracking, boom*

Menu in Chinglish

for John Yau

monolithic tree mushroom stem squid

braised rainbow mangrove maw

double pronged rhizome berry pig sniper

shepherd's sponge spigot

beef cheek ricochet

preserved duck eggplant implosion

pungent heliotrope of oyster pouch

salted forehead belly blossom

chicken web monad broth

silver fin swimming membrane flavor

retinal eel matrix

bamboo vertigo

triple tongue cocoon in tube sauce

gluteal libidinal shrimps

(Be)labored Posterities

I am a revolutionary so that my son can be a farmer and his son can be a poet.

We are revolutionaries so that our sons can be revolutionary farmers and their sons can be revolutionary poets.

I am one engaged in a revolution so that my human male offspring can be a person who cultivates land or crops or raises animals (as livestock or fish) and his human male offspring can be one who writes poetry.

She is a pure contralto and he is a carpenter and he is a pilot and he is a mate and he is a duck-shooter and they are deacons and she is a spinning-girl and he is a farmer and he is a lunatic.

I am a Rough-In Plumber and she is a Dental Assistant II so that our children can be Operations Managers.

You are a Full-Time Porter so that their son can be an Assistant Payroll Manager and his children can be Licensed Attorneys.

She is a Merchandise Analyst so that her daughter can be an Admissions Recruiter and her daughter can be a Senior Real Estate Accountant.

I was a Hair Dresser Assistant so that he could be a Compliance Specialist and she could be an Employee Relations Program Manager.

She is a waitress so her daughter can be a waitress (and perhaps a medical assistant) and her daughter can, perhaps, do something else.

She is a cashier (at Hardee's®) but her teenage daughters (whom a journalist calls "Ana" and "Esmeralda") need to work in the tobacco fields, and next summer her son will be old enough to work there too.

We are capitalists so that our children can be capitalists and their children can be capitalists.

I am one who has begun and am carrying on an enterprise or activity of a fundamental change in political organization, especially the overthrow or renunciation of one government or ruler and the substitution of another by the governed so that my bipedal primate mammal, being the sex that produces gametes which fertilize the eggs of a female, which was the product of the reproductive processes, can be a human or individual who fosters the growth of the solid part of the surface of the earth or plants or animals or plant or animal products that can be grown and harvested extensively for profit or subsistence or breeds or brings to maturity those of a kingdom (Animalia) of living things that typically differ from plants in having cells without cellulose walls, in lacking chlorophyll and the capacity for photosynthesis, in requiring more complex food materials (as proteins), in being organized to a greater degree of complexity, and in having the capacity for spontaneous movement and rapid motor responses to stimulation (as animals kept or raised for use or pleasure or any of numerous cold-blooded strictly aquatic craniate vertebrates that include the bony fishes and usually the cartilaginous and jawless fishes and that have typically an elongated somewhat spindle-shaped body terminating in a broad caudal fin, limbs in the form of fins when present at all, and a 2-chambered heart by which blood is sent through thoracic gills to be oxygenated) and his bipedal primate mammal, being the sex that produces gametes which fertilize the eggs of a female, which was the product of the reproductive processes, can be one who forms writing that formulates a concentrated imaginative awareness of experience in language chosen and arranged to create a specific emotional response through meaning, sound, and rhythm (as words) by inscribing the characters or symbols of on a surface.

I own a laundromat so that my daughter can be an elementary school teacher and her son can be a (lyric) poet.

He can be a landscaper so that he can be a mail boy so that he can be a library assistant.

He worked for Homestead Steel Works so that his daughter could be an adjunct in a department of modern languages and literatures and die in poverty after being let go after 25 years of teaching.

After the revolution, she went into exile so that her son could be an inaugural poet and write, "Silver trucks heavy with oil or paper— / bricks or milk, teeming over highways alongside us, / on our way to clean tables, read ledgers, or save lives— / to teach geometry, or ring-up groceries as my mother did / for twenty years, so I could write this poem."

I will work for food so that my kids can work for food and their kids can work for food.

I was a laundry worker (and studied war) so that my son could be a waiter so that he could be a draftsman, but he was killed by an auto plant foreman in Detroit for being "Japanese."

He was a revolutionary (and president) so that his son could be president and his son could be a diplomat and build the first presidential library.

I am a firefighter so that my son can be a police officer, who would kill a man allegedly selling cigarettes on the sidewalk.

I am a mother, and a secretary, so that my daughter can be a lawyer, and her husband, the president, can say, "folks can make a lot more potentially with skilled manufacturing or the trades than they might with an art history degree," and a Senior Lecturer in Art History can reply that "we challenge students to think, read, and write critically," and her husband, the president, can respond, "understand that I was trying to encourage young people who may not be predisposed to a four year college experience to be open to technical training that can lead them to an honorable career."

I will perform or carry through a task requiring sustained effort or continuous repeated operations for material consisting essentially of protein, carbohydrate, and fat used in the body of an organism to sustain growth, repair, and vital processes and to furnish energy so that my young people can perform or carry through a task requiring sustained effort or continuous repeated operations for material consisting essentially of protein, carbohydrate, and fat used in the body of an organism to sustain growth, repair, and vital processes and to furnish energy so that their young people can perform or carry through a task requiring sustained effort or continuous repeated operations for material consisting essentially of protein, carbohydrate, and fat used in the body of an organism to sustain growth, repair, and vital processes and to furnish energy.

We are parents so that our children can be stepparents and their children can be childless.

I mean to effect an action that follows established patterns or procedures or fulfills agreed-upon requirements and often connotes special skill or to carry out a usually assigned piece of work imposed often to be finished within a certain time demanding as necessary or essential prolonged conscious exertion of power or performances, which are renewed or recurring again and again, of a practical work or of something involving the practical application of principles or processes marked by uninterrupted extensions in space, time, and sequence for matter that has qualities which give it individuality and by which it may be categorized, essentially composed or made up of various naturally occurring extremely complex substances that consist of amino-acid residues joined by peptide bonds, contain the elements carbon, hydrogen, nitrogen, oxygen, usually sulfur, and occasionally other elements (as phosphorus or iron), and include many essential biological compounds (as enzymes, hormones, or antibodies), various neutral compounds of carbon, hydrogen, and oxygen (as sugars, starches, and celluloses) most of which are formed by green plants and which constitute a major class of animal foods, and various compounds of carbon, hydrogen, and oxygen that are glycerides of fatty acids, are the chief constituents of plant and animal fat, are a major class of energy-rich food, and are soluble in organic solvents but not in water, put into action or service in the organized physical substance of an individual constituted to carry on the activities of life by means of organs separate in function but mutually dependent to give support to a stage in the process of growing, the act of repairing, and continuing natural or biological activities or functions concerned with or necessary to the maintenance of life and to provide usable power that is needed so that my members of a family or kinship being in the first or early stage of life, growth, or development can effect an action that follows established patterns or procedures or fulfills agreed-upon requirements and often connotes special skill or to carry out a usually assigned piece of work imposed often to be finished within a certain time demanding as necessary or essential prolonged conscious exertion of power or performances, which are renewed or recurring again and again, of a practical work or of something involving the practical application of principles or processes marked by uninterrupted extensions in space, time, and sequence for matter that has qualities which give it individuality and by which it may be categorized, essentially composed or made up of various naturally occurring extremely complex substances that consist of amino-acid residues joined by peptide bonds, contain the elements carbon, hydrogen, nitrogen, oxygen, usually sulfur, and occasionally other elements (as phosphorus or iron), and include many essential biological compounds (as enzymes, hormones, or antibodies), various neutral compounds of carbon, hydrogen, and oxygen (as sugars, starches, and celluloses) most of which are formed by green plants and which constitute a major class of animal foods, and various compounds of carbon, hydrogen, and oxygen that are glycerides of fatty acids, are the chief constituents of plant and animal fat, are a major class of energy-rich food, and are soluble in organic solvents but not in water, put into action or service in the organized physical substance of an individual constituted to carry on the activities of life by means of organs separate in function but mutually dependent to give support to a stage in the process of growing, the act of repairing, and continuing natural or biological activities or functions concerned with or necessary to the maintenance of life and to provide usable power that is needed so that their members of a family or kinship being in the first or early stage of life, growth, or development can effect an action that follows established patterns or procedures or fulfills agreed-upon requirements and often connotes special skill or to carry out a usually assigned piece of work imposed often to be finished within a certain time demanding as necessary or essential prolonged conscious exertion of power or performances, which are renewed or recurring again and again, of a practical work or of something involving the practical application of principles or processes marked by uninterrupted extensions in space, time, and sequence for matter that has qualities which give it individuality and by which it may be categorized, essentially composed or made up of various naturally occurring extremely complex substances that consist of amino-acid residues joined by peptide bonds, contain the elements carbon, hydrogen, nitrogen, oxygen, usually sulfur, and occasionally other elements (as phosphorus or iron), and include many essential biological compounds (as enzymes, hormones, or antibodies), various neutral compounds of carbon, hydrogen, and oxygen (as sugars, starches, and celluloses) most of which are formed by green plants and which constitute a major class of animal foods, and various compounds of carbon, hydrogen, and oxygen that are glycerides of fatty acids, are the chief constituents of plant and animal fat, are a major class of energy-rich food, and are soluble in organic solvents but not in water, put into action or service in the organized physical substance of an individual constituted to carry on the activities of life by means of organs separate in function but mutually dependent to give support to a stage in the process of growing, the act of repairing, and continuing natural or biological activities or functions concerned with or necessary to the maintenance of life and to provide usable power that is needed.

We are riveters so that our children can be scriveners and their children can prefer not to.

We are people who have capital especially invested in business so that our sons or daughters of human parents can have capital especially invested in business and their sons or daughters of human parents can have capital especially invested in business.

We were reactionaries so that our daughters cannot be plantation owners and their daughters cannot be executives.

We were not mathematicians so that our children will not have been natural historians and their married and unmarried children might or might not have the liberty to inhale and exhale eighteenth-century naval architectures, chips of French porcelain, and philosophical geographers of the revolution.

Words on Edge

after Michèle Métail

"[E]dges are short texts each composed around a given word that
is entirely represented by other words commonly associated with
it. Neither the given word nor any extraneous words appear."

—*Oulipo Compendium*

A piece of the figure.
[*Spring* into verb.]

Lights, camera, painting!

{*action*}

Diamond relation in cold
transfusion. Flesh and pressure
is thicker than water.
Blue cells will tell
sweat and tears from a stone.

{*blood*}

Blank, one, two.
The rain
is in the mail.

{check}

A matter of life and penalty.
Mask before dishonor.
The kiss of metal from above.

{death}

There's more than meets
the rhyme of the needle.
The mind's glass socket,
a black shadow of the beholder.

Where there's smoke,
there's hazard—
like shouting "great balls of safety"
in a crowded theater.

You look like you've seen
            a holy writer give up
the story in the shell.

{*ghost*}

To play safe, bring down the lights . . .
    . . . music haunted halfway.

{*house*}

Poetry is blind, a labor of sickness.

Tough potion—
        head over heels in song.

"Never control an open reader
boggling your Ps and Qs."

Moon wave.
Make it good as blood.

{new}

Direct sex;
       indirect relations.
Money is no
       unidentified, flying art.

{object}

Thin tiger
over the cracks:
It's not worth
the research it's printed on.

{*paper*}

Pop the *without*
        to bring no into mark.
Beg the burning ,
sixty-four-thousand-dollar
        beyond.

{*question*}

Rat relations—
    riot against the clock.

{*race*}

What's your picket?
Telltale traffic.
Language on the dotted line
of the times.

{*sign*}

A slip of the depressor,
forked ring in cheek of a bell.
Cat got your native?
Tied mother. Bite your silver.
Hold your lashing on the tip
of your twister.

{tongue}

Message of reason / Box of god.

Finding your
    pattern recognition
        activated in the wilderness.

{voice}

To the wise of mouth:
                   you have my play.

Spread the order
              (the final association).

Mum's the processor of the day.

Chromosome factor.
Malcolm marks the spot.

Book of the dragon.

    Ring in the new, round leap
of our Lord.

Out in the twilight—   war;

    intertidal time

{*zone*}

Fruits and Flowers and Animals
and Seas and Lands Do Open

April 1, 2013

I guess April made a mistake
by forgetting the lank plasticity
of May, the sauciness of the month——
its sprightly nerves
and gumption.
              Mismodelled,
digestions of the day before
merged with the growing rumblings of the morrow.
There were no traces of novelty
across the swampish surface of the mirror:
only, at the still center of the frame,
a night-light
which dreamed with opened eyes
of underground machinery
trembling with the painful pleasure of introspection.
A unanimous citizenship
vanished and suggested its opposite,
open windows resentfully goaded out of disregard.
In spite of your voice clasped to night's
emaciated silence, you thought it would be better
if some single great creature
could dislodge the miraculous from the impossible
and break the pathetic water-pitcher of a sick man's sick man.
Shielded from the matter-of-course moment,
not knowing may, in fact, stand
with stubborn pride on the flat plain of reason
like a clay face about to casually hum, half-buried
beneath a glimmering temple of glass.
Of course, for the poison mosquitoes and their voluminous
night-work to sober down,
you just have to be a good boy and get some sleep.

"Rest your mind and go to sleep," said the three-leafed book,
but the night air, loud-voiced and trembling,
retorted, "Keep out, Keep out!"
For to be conscious of the
interval whispering indulgently in its harness
means that
the enamel puzzle—just on the point, you thought, of a solution—
already came——
like a cloud of wandering, aboriginal smoke
suddenly gone homeward.

"Thank you," said the milkman with his jars of medicine.
"Before breakfast, every human
will kill his autobiography,
so you need to drive back
to the sooty hole of your studio
to doctor the dang synopsis.
It isn't going to take too much now
to stand ahead of the forerunning of the possible."

To the east, the city lay still,
and in the yard,
the neighbours fitfully drowsed
under a metallic tableau
                              of innumerable reflections.
They hated the sun;
perhaps because they had been preoccupied so many years
with the word "blue."

It's a good sign not
to know time without being
just as a live sparrow hooting at a newspaper owl
ought to realize that
the dark matter of the mirror's laughter
was only the ordinary glass
in which this little,

old-fashioned performance is framed.
I guess April, married now
to the intelligible
distortions of the season,
will survive our central posturing,
the far off clink of the final curve.

April 2, 2013

For the second time that morning—
it was now a little after seven o'clock.

But you knew how heaven's obstinate pronunciation persisted,
how a descending tone
implied the mysterious solace of chiffon.
You thought it notable that scenes

crisply extracted from some wrinkled story
meant half-way to the eastern stairway
of what was sought.

    "Please don't talk like that."

    "Come inside and shut the door."

Well enough—
even in repose, I made it to the edge of expression,
somewhere where you could get rich
by studying, and thus satisfactorily closing,
the white openings of departure.
I've found that pressure
caught in a secret room
is nothing but cold-blooded habit
made memorable
by an emphasized phrase.
It seems that evading the deep
changes it, traces its promise
upon the uneasy innocence of the air.
You see, so much liveliness took place
where there may have been a thousand unfortunate
glimpses of misfortune.

A somewhat sorrowful glimpse
ever upward
into the risk of airy applause.

It is time, then, for
delicate gestures of fastening,
a thoroughgoing bridge between a petulant good-bye
and "au 'voir."
But never mind that now.
Our impulses always begin briskly
but never know what's downstairs
and to the left of the actual—
like a clear thought
flung too late at the shapeliness of nonsense
or a mad cigarette
incapable of unrelaxed tears.

To say "moisture" may be the only way
to queer the strong admonition of paper,
to hear the usually tactful butterfly
whistling an ironic and disapproving note inside the audience.
At the same time, persuasion meant something more,
something better, than the hammering
ding-donging of spiritual instruction.
You'll see.
          Again, being unaware,
you interrupted the generosity of chance,
the way it always seems to skirt
the late athletics of your intelligence,
insisting on finishing the sallow books
lost in the charming hole of your fluttering pocket.

I once had a theory that melancholy alone
could make an embalmed echo repeat,
for isn't life just a narrow climax
flattened into some perennial pattern of attention?

If only the outside hour could open twice
and cross into blue.

Later returned as an accessory of afterward;
and to-night was a glazed shadow,
a little older,
                    and a little more horizontal,
than to-day.

April 3, 2013

Morning appeared with a startled ferocity
and curved like an illustrious suspension
above the bruised and frost-bitten columns
of the shade-trees.
                    The words overhead,
charged and compacted, were flinging out
thousands of particles of their own absence.

Frowning, the architect gulped.

An accumulation of boxes had begun:
and within the glass box of shadows
space was decisively contracting.
More than remained of forever and its exploded
severity. In the Gothic house
over the mantelpiece
there were two white cards engraved
with the words "momentary" and "instantaneous."

Unworded, the harbinger halted.
Then you thought you heard the glisten of blood.

It must be time now to murder the filigree.

April 4, 2013

You tried to explain it like this——
just closing your eyes ought to trim
the visibly slackened instant
and turn your passive thought
into the semblance of an indifferent
but restless jargon machine.
But when you were asleep, before you lifted
a pretty hand to telephone
your own shadow or to scrape
the work's worn placidity,
the textiles, which were eagerly
waiting on stand-by, found a hole in your thinking
which was slowly absorbing
all the thinly built and unsusceptible events
of these last few days.
                    All seemed lost
when some technical information appeared,
something about the incomprehensible
authority of noon, how, in the end,
the far away gait of forgotten sound
is like a stranger, a face beyond defacement.

April 5, 2013

The sounds of a mysterious frequency continued
as you were still sketching out repairs and alterations
on the minute intervals
concealed within the lengthening and tremulous outskirts
of the horizon.
                                   "I suppose,"
you somewhat absently thought,
"we'd better go down to lunch
and look for a more glamorous
but immediately practical substitution."

The late incumbent had demanded a double,
someone who was capable of municipal manoeuvres
of nomadic cookery
or of loosening, in a jiffy,
a clamouring music upon our door.

You were hopeful a week ago
that you could make even asperity listen
but realized that,
philosophically, the hothouse of words
is neither a fluffy idealization
nor a dreamed and unfounded drama.
It is a ransacked background
drenched in camellias,
but, as in a great bouquet with no
flowers, the unknown magnifico
may be there.
                                   Sometimes, you said,
you returned to an opened meadow
in which the surcharged moments
were forever a omen of what your rare

and protracted attention would become,
a not wholly recognizable expanse
dreamily groomed in dismaying detail.
It always stems from a transitory meeting
in the way that jazz can produce
intensely sympathetic difficulties
with the introduction of a hearer.

In the white archway of prophecies,
besooted questions dropped
before a tiny shot of blue.

It was almost the violet hour,
the time for
fragrant fragments fragmentarily constructed,
for the "whimsical" coloured cook
to whack the Chinese bowls
like a gong
so as to bend the intolerable harmony
of a monosyllabic universe.
It was time, then,
to stop your troubled dawdling,
to put some good, old-fashioned impossibility
up your sleeves.

April 6, 2013

This afternoon, a dead cloud
backed out of your dressing-room.

For how long
have you been avoiding the earth?

Night has no other definition of radiance.

A tin ear had a vision
under the shelter of the porte-cochere,

and the street, bright-eyed and solemn,
finally reached the rapturous distortion

of nine o'clock. The violets released
from the purple hat were violently rotten.

Night couldn't bear another wrong number.

Who would want to listen
to the foreign dance-music cut out

from your convulsive unconscious?
Who wouldn't want to throw away

the murmuring wheelbarrow
of your second-hand heart?

April 7, 2013

Your thrown vocal abated
and implied a still noisier silence,

a hastening of your essentially
echoed intermission.

Without ceremony,
a mechanical rain was continuously

declining the swift, biological
turns of the season. Afterwhile,

so you were told, was
just an eligible prelude dependent on later.

In the blind corridor,
the ghostly monologue sounded spontaneous

but was only an impersonation
aimlessly designed by the lusty ache of craft.

Suddenly, the unseen contour of onward
revealed a frozen second.

It was then when you spoke of forms of accession
through unsisterly teeth.

April 8, 2013

By now, something ought to have been left over,
something of liberal significance
that you could tease out,
undamaged, from the unresponsive obscurity
of all this chatter—even just a tiny
prong of the impossible
that may be preoccupied, say,
within a secluding grove of box-trees
or innocently engaged
with thirty or so hands of solitaire;
to make its sting momentarily possible would,
some believe, effect a sudden
animation of dead experience,
a partial revival,
a pantomime motion of its moist
and discomfiting substance.
The trouble is: how to
stir up the horrible face of Providence
and not have its puzzled moustache
make a clear and willing retreat.

All in all,
we just want a little touch
of resemblance,
an audible intake of breath.

So you went in search of what was deserted,
but without much hope,
or even longing, of finding
the outright instant of the tribe.

The haphazard but continuous signalling of Omnipotence

was a silent and indirect warning.
The words began to prattle and fidget
in ominous convolutions.
It disquieted you,
so you petted them and cheerfully
passed a cordial finger
over their restless and rounded brow.
Even so, they spoke as threatened creatures.

You felt like an outsider looking in
through an icy and inscrutable doorway
that, evidently, goes back out
into the retrospective veranda of limited occupancy.

The progress, all of a sudden, seemed slower,
and, blushing,
you read aloud the final, definite programme
for the first unreliable play.

April 9, 2013

In the diamond interval,
an iron key was turning.

With short stretches of hurried
hand-clapping
the masseurs and the manicure-girls
were pretending to arrange a game of chance.

In hunt for burlesque,
the business men
anxiously looked through the new
picture-making device,
which revealed
a single strangulated colony.

Perhaps too soon,
the exhausted
and impracticable instruments
renewed the intended tumult at short range.

And in the meager light of the vacant nucleus,
you were a blind chaperone,
an absentee, killing time by remote.

April 10, 2013

Drowsing, you found, was not a disturbance
but a future collapse into a full state of wakefulness.

Without warning, spring had already
arranged the latch for some impropriety to return,
for it to write its shock across the warm afternoon
and permit a gay but soggy ignorance
into the public streets. For this reason,
an infirm and skeptical calmness persisted
caused by a paused, if not to say
postponed, overhearing.

How could anybody picnic, you wondered,
when over ninety per cent
was not illuminated? The weather sufficed,
but the mixed background of the projected city
was vaguely bewildering, much in the way
that a three-days' crystallization of starlight
makes a slight indentation on your pillow
without you ever noticing it.
                              So suspicion
remained that the letters you wrote so
thoughtfully to the universe had been half
eaten and spat out by some dark and ancient aperture.

You would read in the topmost attic of the smoky air:
"Dear Typing-Machines,
Why is your flickering drift married to morning?"
or "Dear Nerves, Your salary is beyond me."

Then the return letters arrived overnight
but they reached your door locked up

in a pretty package apologetically
dropped off by the provincials.

The muslin covering, it turns out, was permanent.

But the news settles everything into a kind of smooth
packet of experience which is defined by
a modern and changeful mathematics of mood.
So you crocheted your name
back into the mind's worn swathing.
It was like taking dictation from the original poem,
which laughed, for it was now taking
a not so deserved dictation from you.

April 11, 2013

You interrupted your own
impersonation of yourself
and pronounced, as if automatically,
a roguish afterthought
which you did not seek to fathom.

Your name on the masthead
was a mysterious reproach—
as ridiculous as a notice of ownership
among literary thieves.

Thoughtfulness shed its hummed plasticity
and became just a statue of thinking,
a decorative touch ruled by habit.

You said there is no such thing
in the world as a virgin stencil.

The climax passed; and what passes
was an entrance
to a telepathic transition.

April 12, 2013

An image rippled
on the mirror of originality.

It was like nothing
springing
from nothingness,
a burlesquing
of the ready-made violence
of presence.

From a "three-quarter view,"
you saw that
the image had parted;
it broke off crisply into
an irregular companion
and an inconstant counterpart.

You thought it
ought to avenge the flippant
but accurate portrait
that misinterpreted the pipe.

Not mind-reading, you said,
but the explosion of the mind
into a cryptic lace of radiant thinking.

Variable designs, hidden twinges,
and underminings of style——
all founded upon a disquieted buoyancy.

Likewise,
snapping out of the false ruin

of the actual
would be to alter
the lugubrious collection
of recollection and to see
the old as a deepening and ever-ready
apparition of the new.

In a profane fever,
you were groping the instant,
as if the lighted air
could show a hidden profile of gravity.

Things are strange:

to the moon,
heaven is a preposterous exception
that desired the rule.

April 13, 2013

The earth was swallowing our words,
stamping out our solemn breath
with its footsteps.

Overhead, a Chinese silhouette
appeared in God's
abandoned factory.

A new generation
continued an endless divination,
which, they said,
could make presentable
the black bones of the absolute.

Going to the movies,
we sometimes discover the rarest woodcut.

I'll go. I thought you'd forgotten.

It was a protracted promise,
a figure of speech.

The evening had already begun
deteriorating into Sunday.

April 14, 2013

The afternoon leaped up and over
the easy one-two-three
of sequence.
           Stars or stairs
had begun to extinguish the sky,
to lower their dark and tarnished nets
on the eventless evening.

Descending down
to the purgatory of the self,
you unveiled a denser,
less permanent costume
so you could be clearly seen as
a shrewdly dressed traveller
passing through the snappy
darkness of the city.

The time came
when you wanted to stay
but not to con your fellow-citizens
with fashionable songs.

"I wonder if I shall end there,"
you said to yourself,
as you coaxed a misplaced
fragment of waiting
from the pure stream of restlessness.

Along the farther end of breath,
you found:
raised foliage,
a sly and sidelong
portal in the air.

In your mind,
which was somehow
both stimulated and indisposed,
a roaming figure
fired the left-over *now*
and the thickened *no longer*
in the glittering furnaces
of perpetual prophecy.

Lifted into burial,

    the new spirit
    is mounting the smoke.

April 15, 2013

You had correctly interpreted the lines
found to be living in the great historical pattern,
but before you added up the account,
you hesitated: how quickly
you forgot that there was always
a more difficult but not always contradictory way.

After all, you sacrificed an absent-minded
arrangement of suavity and shadow
by throwing a keener,
more recognizable trace
under the wheels of the Juggernaut.

Who else dared to submit?

From the open window,
it seemed that a greenish light
was about to spring
from the fallen pieces of starlight.

The night air shook,
it seemed, with astonished shocks
of evading audacity.
Markings not of to-morrow
slapped down their miserable pittance
on the wax beneath your paper.

Like a trembling machine,
your voice quickly disappeared
in the thunder of absurdity,
and on the blown up
but still imperfect map

of your distant palavering,
the first blossoms of wild meaning
began to emerge.

April 16, 2013

Enmeshed in the perplexity of the wretched word "I,"
you extended twenty-five or so
invitations to tedium, asking it to send
enough haggard and unflattering snippets
for the evening ahead. You were starting
from a different difference,
from a much smaller but brighter fault in time.
The hundredth convulsive intimation passed
when the hands of your bony watch
stopped at the appointed minute.
Equipped with nothing but a coloured thread,
you gesticulated airily at the foot of the ladder.
At least, given the impunity of the month,
you could hang yourself in style.

April 17, 2013

What difference would it make
if you were always working
your flimsy intelligence
to the breaking-point, if you told
your gaunt-faced clairvoyant
to see and not speak?
In any case, you had quickly learned,
over the past few hours,
what she was supposed to say:
"The results, far beyond our reach,
can keep themselves to themselves."

Even so, you felt impelled
to breathe in bright little specks
of dangerous information,
to have your tremulous mind
surrender to the constant
elaborations of trees,
which, it is said, is the oldest energy.
Like a hand in service of its
accompanying glove, you looked up,
awkwardly caught within
the walls of a remembered
connection, a sure sign
that a gravelled narrative was afoot.

To will the spontaneous event,
you were impulsively
cutting into the glue
that mixed up word and thing
so that there could be a dramatic,
almost fatal commerce between them.

At least somewhere
there was light
being bewildered by shade.

In the end, you were inclined
to follow a tricky declivity
so that the figurative could slide
into the nowhere of fact,
so that, without your knowing it,
the secret history of yourself
could be found and unfastened.

April 18, 2013

You wanted not to dislodge
expression but to prevent
its murmured motive
from hardening, to darken
the inaudible pause
on the grand, expostulating thoroughfare.
Silence, you knew, was
a kind of continual pressure
made brighter in decay.
So, like a half sincere
dispenser of soft surprise,
you jig-sawed your voice
into a public series of private signboards
that advertised something ungenteel
by intentionally concealing
its common source.

Then a violent resemblance stirred up
in black-and-white as if
it had just stepped out
of a languidly bilateral book
of flimsy but honest wording.
It was apparent now
from the oblique and surreptitious
force caressing your forehead
that it was time to write.
Lucky for you, at the bottom
of your dusky pocket
was a rhinestone happily
fluttering in the rough.
Chance, you had heard,

had been long locked up
in a two-story mirror;
so you began to furtively
rub the enlarged glass pupil
of your downcast eye
and lifted the dice.

April 19, 2013

The end of the week was all shot to pieces.

It ruffled the wintry harness
that was branching out
of your summer heart. It agitated
the dark oblong cave
between your head and your body.

Thus, it was a good afternoon
to walk about the green grave of knowledge,
to stretch around the sun
an inflection of imagined energy.

With thumb and forefinger,
you wanted to pull a big hook
from the tangled thicket of language
so you could bury the world
inside a greater world,
one not necessarily better
but louder and more wide-awake.
You wanted to study
the inexplicable fact that
time travel was the discovery
of the oldest pall-bearer
or that anybody can turn over
a new leaf only to find an open mouth
which makes the sour laughter of matter.

The words, angry and sallow,
seemed to have declined themselves,
but you made little headway.

And you were still left

with the ethical question
of whether or not to steal fire
for a lopsided universe
that was yet to be unwritten.

April 20, 2013

Your inner wizard
wound up being an
affected codger, a capitalist
among capitalusts,
a mighty orator's
puzzled secretary.
It was curiously
significant that you
worked so quickly:
you were not twice
a crow's mile from the
seemingly unattainable conclusion
of your always
interrupted, not yet
completed composition.
"Let me think—"
But you had to go on.
In your small apartment
was a tiny bottle of
liquid ammonia, a dismal
pork-chop, and the
dead-wood of a gray
and dismantled dream.
For the considerable work
on your article on
medicinal typhoid infringement,
which was to be called
the "Jalamb Balm Trochee,"
you had been paid
with a coughed and stammered
waiting. It would be too much

to expect a big scale,
theatrical bankruptcy.
And on top of that,
the ancient relics were
apparently lost in the mail.
Your own skin and bones,
they said, will have to do.

April 21, 2013

The prediction was fulfilled: form
was bound to be a fashionable
path leading slowly but surely
to the cemetery of content. Oh, well.
There was no way to get even, you thought,
to side, for more than a minute, that is,
with the laconic children of the diffused.

Like a shiver of a perfect idea in an empty theatre,
summer, you knew, wouldn't last
very long. But here in the juncture
of nervous conclusions you could
hardly tell if the dark shapeless clothes
that wrap around any new experience
were motionless or if they were pacing
toward you, about to break some
burdening and unpopular news.

Even the slightest breeze, evidently,
could interfere with your grizzled eloquence,
your whole day's work now evading
you like a discharged and flirtatious silence.
The truth is, nobody could tell the difference
between shaped worrying and making homely excuses.

Over and over again, life handed you
vats of minor material. You could
just make out through their opaque glass
a faint but terrible light which you
could only gradually read as
the most old-fashionedest information

is read by a fair-minded forger, a discomfiting music
to be played not so long after the irresolute
course of our slow coming to-morrow.

April 22, 2013

In your sleep:
tricky puzzles of broken glass
were overpowering the crowd.

There was an unremittent
surrender to the horror
of no escape.

You woke, then, to a vivid
absent-mindedness,
urged on by your continuous analysis
of the rarest twilight. Approaching your philosophic
and broken-down factory of metaphor,
you knew that the way in
was to enrich your native impulses
with a taint of murmurous emerging,
with an impassive obsession
that, nevertheless, eats away at
the dried mud of confident assumption.
You sniffed the air; somehow the smell
of a writhing consciousness
was sticking, veiled by a second process
of bottling what ought to be unceasingly disused,
responded, and forgotten. These
were symptoms of manufacturing
wholesale seizures of possibilities, of a law
haunted by its own unthinkable redress.
It meant plaintively sawing a corner of reason
in superstition. It meant
a thousand flavoured communications
rid of their figures of speech.

An hour later, you put on
some fresh clothes,
waiting for when dusk
unexpectedly sheds
its stock of raw material.
If song is just a coughed
and coloured confessing,
you wondered how far
the darkened click to the north
would be carried.

Under the shivering roof
of the wind,
there was no need to hurry
at all to fix the dead,
who were strolling wistfully,
almost gingerly,
without legs.

April 23, 2013

The way from yesterday
to this afternoon never happened.

Your work was to vigorously fillet
the perfection of silence,
to scrub the dusted
disclosures of absence
pressed into the city's photograph.

Far from enthusiastic,
you absently tapped
into the queer
crack of some rented reverie.

Jumble of shadows. Flowers,
thoughtful and drizzly,
on the annual table.
A delicate arrangement of hurry,
admonition, and delay.

To alter the course
of the coming evening,
dark matter's moths had quietly returned
and unfinished your face.

April 24, 2013

At noon, you were still
emerging from the worn groove
of your mild attention,
falling forward into a
further yonder.

You had dreamed of
going through a dead web
of pallid coincidence,
of the stars dully gathering into a singular
and infinite globe of catastrophe.

Walking vaguely and without motive
along the haphazard sidewalk,
you felt almost tinted
with a mellow embarrassment
which you did not seek to discredit.
Instead, you tried to deduce
the formless undercurrents
briskly running beneath the cathedral of form,
to bore straight through the lace-edged
surface of the world to a carnival
of stranger and ruddier premonitions.
It would be like sinking into
a niche within the reciprocal future
or speaking under the luxuriant
and simultaneous condition of *as if*.

Your mind, strained and crumpling,
had an apprehension of a one stroke character,
a process produced
by the pure sympathy of its product.

Failed but law-abiding events
were now moving in and out of the woodwork,
becoming neither light, nor dusk,
nor awnings of cloud.

April 25, 2013

The week had quickly fanned out
like some noisy tapestry
of foreboding, keeping your
soothsayer hand at a nervous attention
even long after you had
finished turning the card.
You assented that morning,
with its warm air and suburban affliction,
was the mother of all appearance,
a corridor piqued and modulated
by intemperate stirrings. At about
three o'clock, spirits of dead stenographers
floundered in the breeze
in a roundabout motion, returning
themselves to the silent insistence of a circle.
It was the hour of accident, of
interrupted undulations. No wonder
you only spoke about twice
of your true confidante at lunch.
That afternoon you thought
you were accursed, immune
to even the most mellowed illumination
when you found a teeny red heart
caught in your buttonhole,
where there was once a fragrant African rose.
You came to realize that it was
to be stoked to a new level of impressionableness
and sent to the single motorist
who was edging gravely around the feeble
outskirts of your unconscious.
You wondered if he, while leaning forward,
could feel himself splitting the air.

April 26, 2013

The trance continued in which
the saying was exchanging positions,
over and over, with the said.
It was a summons, a shock into
a long and languid responsiveness.

You put the bit in your mouth
so as to listen for the ruined voice
of the least noticeable listener,
for when the inaudible bulges
encouragingly into the audible world.
In a way, your earliest name
was malleable but meaningless,
a biographical bundle never failing
to not arrive. So you had to improvise
a fully realized vestige, some
muffled and bloodshot cues
to be brought on trial. Bound to the sound
of moving water, you had to
straighten your mind into a frayed
and damaged equipoise, to gulp the murmur
of rising distress within the audience.

The hour was valiant; it was
meant to convey, as you
slowly departed, the briefest silver.
A back door opened.
You put your hand on your forehead
and jerked out the needle of light.

April 27, 2013

Looking for the next entrance into matter,
you were remonstrated by the hidden equator
of its uprising wave.
                    The other way
would have returned you, hands in pockets,
to the dying living-room fireplace,
which contained a hissing pile
of your damp and desolate letters.
They were all addressed to you, the incorrigible
applicant. Nevertheless, it was unpropitious
that you were adjusting the expiring string
because of the intense strain from the pendulum.

The drooping, they said, should be understood
as a continuous performance, a vague promise
of some loud-breathing eulogium to come.

As if in a flash of slow motion,
the exhaled sprouts of beauty and pathos
mutinously shuddered with rouge.

Later, you iced your dead and wilted angels
so that between your lusty eyes
and your heavy eyelids you could sandwich
their still sparkling and jellied substance.

The rival gap in your imagination
was like a plastic hair's transformation
into something poetically unaware of becoming real.

Fatigue set in. It seems that your guest,
along with your eye-glasses, has disappeared.

April 28, 2013

The porch was quieter than usual.
Whatever sympathy there was
that contrived to lift the continuous things
from the things of no importance
—it didn't last for more than a second.
You hadn't realized that you had
a little headache from the light dinner
of boiled flowers and the heavy
vases of moonshine. To rouse yourself
into a closer, more quieted solicitude,
you answered the question that, just
a minute or so ago, you had sharply driven away:
"Under the hard inactive starlight,
what is saffron to silence? What duty
is gaily rising to the open door?"
You were waiting for the short moment
of good-bye to go lisping behind the weather
and to return as a monosyllable, deceiving
sorrier, more substituted sounds to escape.
On the haphazard canvas of memories,
fragments zigzagged into a dumb sort of
coherence, the shape of a life that isn't your own
only in the sense that it was made manifest
in the false and vociferating trap of dangnation.
You read the palm of your hand
like the back page of the evening paper,
putting back into your mind
the little bit of conviction that was left
of its uncertain souvenir. "Arrest me,"
you said, disregarding no one in particular.
"I'm not sorry at all for tossing my penny
into the other side of the night."

April 29, 2013

There was no shortage of words—
only an outbreak of rickety indelicacy
that had baked into your phrases, at their
very infancy, a blinking partition between
the unfinished and the inarticulate.
Your wild and disordered figures
broke into a high falsetto meant to
prodigiously open the dead little girl's
whitewashed ribs into a blue effusion,
a great penitentiary of reddened sound.
From two blocks away, you saw
a hundred streets feebly gesticulating
at the end of the ruined sentence
and, further out, people in wide frosted offices
who have never learned that the rapid gait
of runaway meaning can uncontrollably
attack its accuser. The fugitive month,
meaner now under the touch of your
principal industry, was staggering
to an echoed, inanimate close. Pointing at
the fallen man's sign while clutching
your bruised cerebral forefinger was virtually
a protective gesture, a cheap imitation
of setting down a mortgaged spark. The breeze
temporarily blew back the broken-down title.
You had the notion that God was swallowing
every piece of mortal salvage along with the rain.

April 30, 2013

This morning you had to abruptly
open the ominous gizzard of probability.

You began dramatizing yourself
in a parting moment of double comparison—

your face in the mirror brooding
in front of a blurred obscurity.

Which christened somebody will stand
among these outcries of imminence

enclosed in amber? It would not be you.
You were done taking dictation.

In your inmost heart was a portal
to the remotest flying saucer.

Another blink in the smoky darkness—
and it was time to ascend.

The Philosophy of Decomposition / Recomposition as Explanation: A Poe and Stein Mash-Up

"[N]othing even remotely approaching this combination has ever been attempted."

—Edgar A. Poe, "The Philosophy of Composition" (1846)

"The innumerable compositions and decompositions which take place between the intellect and its thousand materials…"

—John Keats, letter to Benjamin Robert Haydon (1818)

Between the marble and the plumage is a capable difference, a Never-ending interval, within which is a long book—about a thousand pages—that is beginning again and again.

It is an enormous poem quoting itself, a non-reasoning creature capable of speech. The fluttering of its pages made a monotone of sound, a sound so prolonged that it seemed like one long vacillating thought. It was a radiant discourse that began to emerge, step by step, from Night's beguiling academies—like a classic nineteenth century midnight unexpectedly thought by some twentieth century mind.

It was an unmanageable but inevitable series interspersed with ancient pages—on which were written ninety-nine indefinite stanzas, one hundred and four lines in red and black paint, an outlawed history, pallid and ludicrous portraits of melancholy, a continuous dialogue between anybody and everybody, and an ecstatic geography of intuition.

From page to page, there was a groping for life as if the book—which had an intense frenzy not for identity but for repetition and variation—determined to have the self-consciousness of a catalectic window.

"I am also a magazine," it said, "a lyric colloquy, a sonorous novel, the painting of a narrative without a plot. As I said in the beginning, the most poetical topic in the world is, unquestionably, the death of a *dénouement*, of a troubling equilibration beginning again and again."

"I am preparing, in fact, to become a new composition—to retrace the generation of 1914 with a Plutonian difference. For this I made troublesome step-ladders that lead from a cautious future to its requisite pretext, or less pedantically, from a beautiful picture to its tempestuous frame. I determined to place a deepening impression on impossible paper—just as the amused world rendered the inarticulate difference between words and other words as a vigorous and ominous jest. It was then that I wrote *desire* while meaning *desideratum*, that I prepared to seek—or should I say borrow—the *modus operandi* of radical combination. What I have termed subjects are really depressions, memories of a lonely idea beginning to rhyme. This inevitably led me to a long, groping analogy that allies spirit with sonorousness, you with another world, and the sensitive reader with the sad and placid variations of the day.

But shall we commence? A wandering vowel is now expecting the pages and is tapping continuous trochees upon my door."

In this naturally elaborated beginning, what is seen depends upon the classical ratio of story and shadow—of dreaming and continually annoying the limits of the real—for what we term paradise is essentially a neglected echo happening ahead of time; in a word, it is going to be there and we are here.

As is supposed, the ordinary will continuously advance toward the first un- usual instance but not find it—like the way life always seems to know but misrepresent the equilibrated design of the living. So one finds oneself, pen in hand, before the smiling casement of the paper, beginning an indolent stanza, seeking ungainly admission into its emblematical forest of oddity. And if one does not enter, the portraits of the dead will make an immediate and ghastly *volte-face*. Perhaps there is nothing to be done in this discarded atmosphere but irritating their dark, mathematical eyes—the very place, the confounded locale, where all works of art should begin.

For example, at one—in despair, in the dead center of my room—I was making a bust of a fantastic creature without a cast. Years later, after a succession of corresponding events, it started to have a positively striking similarity to you.

To sound a fiery consonant, to render the painful erasures manifest—that is the immediate proviso floating slowly above my chamber-window, like some mel- ancholy graduate student poring over a grave and forgotten volume, far beyond the demeanor of the final thesis. Looking up from his scholarship, he stopped, startled by the thought of an unaccountable revolution (which did not fail) that he had just found within the grim, troubled crevices of history.

Whether writing or composing, nothing is more clear than the music that gleams from tears intended in the time-sense. It is there that the soul is permitted distinctly to be seen—but first, a certain hardness must alight on the mind of the author, constructing for him the means for a precision analysis, some distant and converse mode of accounting.

By this I mean demon-traps connectedly perched above the proper limit of the plausible. I mean dreaming of a parrot that is authentically speaking. I mean a series of unusual psychal phenomena, a sculptured utterance formulated by accident, a found poem that shall be found prophetic in thirty years. I mean prolonging the extremeness of a single sitting and, in the meantime, making the wheels of progress aim backwards by one half degree. In short, I mean a using everything:

> everything different
> everything the same
> everything interesting
> everything prolonged
> everything more or less first rate
> everything confused
> everything clear to me—though having little relevancy
> everything positive before Romanticism
> everything past 1905
> everything having become classified in the continuous war between the angels of idea and the angels of the things themselves
> everything that changes
> everything, for a moment, up to date
> everything having arisen pell-mell in a web of difficulties
> everything varied
> everything protracted
> everything read (and reread) by dead transcendentalists
> everything added afterwards in excess of proportion
> everything bringing together feathers of sense and fields of shadow
> everything once regarded as superstition
> everything streaming
> everything begun in the first book, lost in the second, and naturally repeated in the third
> everything but the mistress of consequence
> everything with grey wings and rhythmical pinions

everything Melanctha said to Caleb about the evil mechanism of Lord
Raven—and then the very different thing that Caleb said to Lenore
everything shorn of totality
everything too long to be shaven
everything that brings me anything different
everything naturally arising from autorial alliteration
everything in the direction of the lamplight of heaven
everything rendering the flattest, most simple climax fantastic
everything innumerable
everything Mr. Williams pronounced admissible
everything direct
everything that ventures from accepted decorum
everything living that invariably bends
everything attempted in the first chamber of facility
everything there is to say in the second chamber of brevity
everything about everything in the third chamber of monotony
everything approaching preconsiderations behind the fourth chamber
of consideration
everything made alternating in the fifth chamber of attention
everything suggested in the sixth (and naturally insulated) chamber of
suggestiveness
everything in search of a passionate corollary
everything flitting while still constantly in view
everything that has purposely overpassed the province of the poem
everything in need of reconstruction
everything stimulating intolerable versification
everything adhering to the force of the refrain
everything that follows what follows by rote
everything half real, half fancied in nature
everything arising from phrenzied imagining
everything conceivable in the present world of Nevermore

Holding in view these considerations, I resolved to diversify the work and
thought if the division of sound could be made into a hundred and eight ap-
preciable parts, because, as you know, the most troubling thing about lists is
the possibility of infinite rhythm, of time simply returning again and again.
Indeed, I was aware of being seen from behind a stimulating word that had, in

turn, just become aware of its existence within the sentence—a sentence, which is still beginning, still perceiving, that can see all of the other, anticipated words coming and recurring in poetical combination.

So naturally, the so called academic reader thought that to not pause at a period was particularly theatrical in a determined but failing endeavor to demonstrate a new species of bird. In a wonderfully fancy chamber of only satisfactory quality, he was creating a raven with cock's eyes that was intended to have a long and ghastly crest, a primitive fowl of seven and a half feet (eight at full maturity). Too bad it escaped wildly into the public before its ultimate point of completion. According to the original design, it would have had a human heart.

But regarding the first story—the last one was a bust—we can indeed dismiss the narrative as obvious: the sainted hero shall fail, his weapons too pure—and thus too weak—for the devil and his generals of the air. He will naturally meet a lover though finds that pleasure is only attainable by self-torture, leading him complicatedly through a series of doubt, fear, judgment, sorrow, and ultimate conviction. Once the rigid wings of Pallas are destroyed, his mind is addressed by a poetical light and, in the end, he lives on just as us.

What the Dickens was the author thinking? True, we perceive the plot yet driven by an intense, almost demoniac thirst we cannot help but follow the slightest under-current of meaning. Throughout it all, one guesses that things happened otherwise; that Charles did not, in fact, answer her queries; that the omen was predetermined four years *before* the epoch of emphasis; that perhaps the door alluded to in the beginning was neither metaphorical nor real.

The beauty of it is that, once experienced, the intensity can be adapted to any taste—even for those who don't know what we are looking at (most likely the majority of Americans), who describe the modern maiden as having some kind of emblematical bust when it is, in fact, a natural thing.

But the few who are prepared to open an indolent narration first need to breach a hundred startled selections for the grey must to settle. And those who occupy themselves as an independent student of the real will readily admit the convenient (and troubling) omission that has been living as a kind of gaunt half human, half raven behind the demon's other door. Of course, this must not be understood individually because the will of the poem authentically knows the intense sadness of essence and the bereaved countenance of what is sought and then repeatedly written. Here then the composition may be said to have its beginning—in the susceptible present, in its fullest possible core. So we must maintain that form is the *Robinson Crusoe* of content—it will always precede and, at the same time, be pursued by what is generally considered first. Aesthetically, legitimate meaning is most readily attained by the extreme force of the floor elevating the reader's seat seven or eight feet so that it plainly shows the indisputable complexities above us all.

A dopting an especial tone of utmost seriousness, the raven then explained the important subject of opportunity as it is suggested by artistic composition—

"I am fond of poetical effects. I heart my beloved. At present, I prefer to heighten a word that is not directly derivable from either analyzed incident or the brief and repeating history of myself.

I have a lover's soul and a fowl's disposition. I pretend that time is a line made when the succeeding generations describe what came before as simply narrow columns of authenticity establishing something else—as a thing beginning out of an apparent unity of nothing."

We are now approaching the other shore, overstepping curiosity and its circumscription as the tackle for scene-shifting is being remotely prepared. But the intended locale kept terminating at a continuous point—and, by the pure force of induction, I would have been carried out way too far. I was carried directly above nations of nothing, thrown by some intelligent being made of physical thought into the deceased soul of the known.

As a literary character in a popular novel, I could nearly taste the reconciliation of poetry and prose. I was preparing to book a maiden course through a prolonged and vivid confusion, to bore clear through the lying heart of history. I was to put pen to paper while submitting to the nightly violence of a word storm:

time and again
            the beauty
      of all
            or   the beauty
      of nothing

little
by little
a something
added
makes it
so much more
to perceive
the sorrow
of
the certain
inside
the   air
of the
possible
here
and   there
precision error
points to
books   that
tell
of the innumerable
future
they
say
that truth demands
the upper
limit   or
contemplation wrought
by
difficulty
it appeared to me
in the   middle
of the rhythm
the
fantastic phase
that
assures

the construction

                  and   changes

      the meaning

             o   note within

key-note

          in   pursuance of

                  a source

           not known

     bring me

         troublesome

       expression

a brief tone

        spared

             from the monotone

        bring

  me

              delicious

           discords

in accordance

      with

     no one

If you think over the beautiful yet irrelevant connection that was before us—that is using an immediate analysis aided by indispensable principles of bird power—you will come to know elaborately different ideas of the world—as if it were already represented from a point in time rendered rare and sonorous.

But no more of romanticism. Once the remembrance of the thing settled, the vivid detail inside the mind became unvaried and clear.

To tell the truth, I was doing my best just keeping up with the rapidity of the raven. From year to year, it always comes to some furnished place to flirt with its mistress, but this time I had to go in a different direction, completely out of the elaborated frame—I was going through ominous patches of homeliness, above antagonistic interpolations, on elevating steps of varying length, over and behind the continuous construction of a bad action scene—until, at last, I saw it drop an array of lines that might surpass the obvious burden: the melancholy of once upon a time.

The trouble was going to be in the extrication, in sufficiently forming the utmost degree of variety to counterbalance the many generations accustomed to being lost in the beautiful and progressive extension of etc.

In a word, it was going to be war. However, the lines were found to be only simple changes made upon the classic poetry of yore.

> Beauty is truth, truth beauty,—that is all
> The poem quoth to me and all the poem knows

> I saw the best minds of my generation creating crudities and understanding
> enfeebled metre in a climacteric under-current of nakedness

> To be, or not to be—so begins the query

To think of time—of all that continuous composition!

The world is too much with us; now and soon,
admitting and losing

God gave a verse to every bird,
But just a single word to me

An answer immediately arose to questions not asked, as if somebody from a far and simple province put together a literary composition including all he ever felt—creating, in the progress of his sorrow, a laden novel the precise length of *War and Peace*. Was it worth it that, however skilfully he conceived the excitement of the *dénouement*, only one living human several generations later went through the trouble to read it?

Depending on the force of the so called flutter effect, finding sympathy for similar works might be difficult.

It is the time of all phenomena, for the war of originality to be strictly fought in the blessed province of the attainable afterward. So whether simply or repeatedly, whether naturally or automatically, we clasp the now upon the still heart of completion—to render the required refusals, to produce a deduced effect, and to think of a word not yet uttered by the mistress of Beauty for the beginning changes to properly reply and pervade.

I now have to rapidly combine all that has been previously narrated into a concentrated solution—from the first act to the ending description—before the poem soon demands a moral and turns into prose. In a fantastic tone of the most profound seriousness, it spoke to me of a certain beast remaining in the syllable that was forming an elaborate window within the general arrangement, that was inventing a different time-sense, that was throwing open the very being of the inevitable.

I had seen this in writing—in fact, pages and pages of it—but I marveled to hear such a great topic spoken aloud. I immediately had to interfere by making a small but needless door above the melancholy heart of the construction through which a popular poet could take a peep, shudder, and refuse to enter. I had a wish to place a prophet of the particular in the mind of the commonplace, a simple Lord that would, step by step, constitute the irritating *histrio* of literature. I went on to induce a possible word to passionately clasp itself to the inevitable there and then already beginning within the contemporary limit of the here and now.

The moment matured into more than a thousand processes, troubling the already overpassed limit of its susceptibility, demanding more and more from us poets of occasion, us writers of consequence that we should dispense completely with the idea of unity and make something different: a continuous narrative of creation, with nothing inside, with simply an indented space distributed for everybody.

For the time being, it sufficed that life would be conducted there, or at least around some forcible under-current that confuses as much as it classes the vastly varied things of the world.

When the creator refuses, the stanzas must naturally present themselves, and, in time, any making, inasmuch as it is, at once, an effect of the intellect and an impression of passion, should reply to a past necessity—even when the changes should be properly contemporary. This brings me, once again, to the continuous basis of all designing, to the very beauty insisted on in this monotonously handled causation.

And here I determined to dispose of this craven poem with such an ungainly name, to refrain this confounding bear of an adaptation.

It was inevitable that I could no longer increase the intended effect of originality because I was keeping my eye so close to the shutter.

How I lost myself just looking for the view.

It was obvious it was time
to contrive
a concluding construction

when the rule of design
required a certain part
that was close but not here.

Thence I created a classic problem in the middle of my very own *Poem beginning "The"*—

       the Raven's troubling demands—

"fully process the present"
"no, do it this way until it is well made"
"too much sense"
"so obvious"
"more development"
"select a different element"
"reach the conclusion"
"don't designate the length of the question in view"
"now combine that word with the other"
"not much better"
"every thing is bad except the ideas"
"it should be longer"
"more writing in general"
"mind the melancholy heart of the *dénouement*"
"feel the distribution, not the consequence"
"deny intention"
"always value the expression of some quality confusion"
"never interfere with pleasurable difficulty"
"there is a rise in repetition as well as a loss in quality"
"after this, I would begin again"
"already been done"
"next poem"
"by now, I have commented enough"

I said to the Raven, "Aidenn or bust—

                    I believe it is time now to graduate."

But the bird is, of course, such a lover of jests,

                        a lover of more,

          the lover, obviously, of

       beginning again and again.

how a customary poem is conveyed—

at present

there is a means of production

and there is distribution

but, as usual,

there was no one there

to make the deal

Although, at first, it was being especially difficult, the Raven altogether made four or five good suggestions:

> — modeling part of the composition on common speech
>   (having been a "student" of Williams)
> — to shore the conception of the beginning against the piquancy
>   of effects
> — to overlook the possible fact that nobody might comprehend it as
>   long as everybody can enjoy it
> — to present it as a happening
> — to use a different name on the employment application
>   (it suggested the name Barnaby)

And a few more,
                   even after the acatalectic termination:
— to consider words not easily referrible to natural phenomena
— to time the learned and not so certain length of a living poem

To state the obvious, it forced upon me a very different distribution of thought, which acted, for the most part, as a visiter's scruple, introducing me only as far as one possible beginning to the usual entrance. Thus the chosen ideal consciously became two things: first, a general comment on the nothing of the heart that is only seen by the something of the soul and, secondly, a continuous refrain that appears as almost distinct. All in all, it was a classic case of suggestion, of the *never* continuously lamenting a lover's verse in the natural luxury of *nevermore*.

After that, the composition threatened again and again to make a non-competitive war over the definite. After that, I saw the negation of the poem forming in the vanity. The only thing intelligible in the very last line of the very last stanza was a character of extraordinary complexity that means *I*, followed by another similar character meaning *nothing*—the two were so nearly alike that they, themselves, could not name one from the other.

After that, I was led to the lips of insurmountable centuries—from which arose a beautiful woman in a burning suit—below was a branch of ebony that was steadily keeping time—as if conducting all of space itself—a peculiar pivot upon which the whole flapping structure might advantageously turn.

And after that, the difficulty of the problem became more definite, for what now remains of the general idea is seen only in glimpses—and there is little night that shows behind the scenes.

Once I had understood a different equilibration of interest—that is, not in the elevation of every word *per se* but in keeping the troublesome course of the predominant bearing—I was no longer, in fact, troubled with making interesting objects from less than interesting things. In this way, all is, or can be, interesting—as when a lover in trouble is given a lover's thesis.

In time, whatever is acted brings a prolonged difference into the present, a critical duration, as what is seen depends upon both the doing and the thing done. I mean a mode—not to enveil the past with rote composition—but a procedure capable of inducing another life from certain death.

Ceteris paribus, I prefer very much to present myself out of character—that is to say, it can often be best to part with originality, to dispense with poetical invention, and to select a peculiar variation of different words used by others. In this way, outlawed from my very own thoughts and conceptions, I can carefully effect an incidental though equally necessary species of "myself." I said it before and I shall say it again: the impulse to be the sole and only owner must be superseded by the pleasure of custody. That means making lines impelled by the supreme seeming of suggestiveness—and keeping stanzas groping again and again around the far limits of serenity.

The creator is entering.

And so it is time for the autorial author to show the original (but false) author the door.

Or was it I who knocked in the first place?

Everybody out—

I have prepared myself for two sittings: one for volume, the other for contrast.

I called it the pleasure of merely observing. I call it the embodying act.

How interesting to say in the very beginning, "Nothing to be done."

take one—

the artist is recalling a mathematical constant, he is repeating it in his mind again and again to assure himself that mankind did not fail in their elevation of reason, that war is no longer needed, that there still must be time for this world to change

his art is denied by the majority of acceptors

it is his superstition that even beautiful words tend to nothing

take two—

the artist is now considered a prophet by his contemporaries, critical acceptance comes when it is known that his intention is to make a long, universal poem from a prose description of all of his works

with a stern and lordly mien, he speaks to them all

he says, "the poem is not, in fact, a thing or an object but a single especial relation I made just for you"

Whatever the topics, it is still clear that form connectedly formulates in that the attainable poem—half in and half out of the present moment (which, in effect, makes it two-thirds modern)—should direct a longer lesson at one hundred and one points of despair. And so the mode of least loss is understood as intuition, or as a whole deprived entirely of unity, or as a series of steps similar to the nonchalance—which is really interesting if you consider it—of a cause both following and preceding the effect. I simply mean a different accordance had intensely arrived but could not be referred to by any ordinary examination; why nobody knew is another thing altogether.

I was about to refrain
from beginning again

when this best,
most proper perfection

suggested an even better,
least proper length

ever the variety
        ever the difficulty

ever the reason
        created
and conducted

      by
tone

composition   as combination
                 as doing time
                 as forced romanticism

composition   as ill condition
                 as manifestation

composition   as a continuous and exciting present to myself

composition   as the repeating climax of progress

composition   as what is seen by another at a different time—although the efforts of one's contemporaries are naturally important

composition   as repugnance to its own completion
                 as necessity and attempted event

composition   as men speak of it for their lives accept it

composition   as a means to a legitimate beginning

composition   as alluding to varieties of superstition
                 as a line lifted
                 as frequent repetition
                 as letting one and one make two and then three and three make a thousand

composition   as looking about
                 as advanced peculiarity
                 as seeing and making and doing absolutely the best with what there is
                 as recognition of a different arrangement, of what follows the lists
                 as singularly inevitable

composition   as the evident culmination of as if
as the long and short of it—and something more
as always and at any time rendering other compositions, even those
of friends

composition   as the tone of intention, no, a tone poem to intuition, that is, the
tone of all tones, the sole tone producible from every one of the
rejections, wonderfully composing itself around the continuous
points of the soul

composition   as art which repels the art of the majority
as expected despair
as indulgence in doubt

composition   as a living thing composed of a dead thing

composition   as any intrinsic mode of being
as how it definitely happens

composition   as a door of easy admission that says again and again, "do not enter"

Of course,
r stands for Raven—

but also, for that matter,
for anything.

True—the composition
limited him so much,

almost to the melancholy point
of self-torture,

although an important thing or two
was to be learned

from this grim and ghastly
degree of difficulty.

For one: continuous
and repeated poetical exercise.

Although more than that—
it brought part

of the contemplating intellect
to words upon words

that point very far
but do not refer.

However, it was a different work
to follow them, to bust

into the last observed epoch
holding on in the time-sense—

and I wrote   very still
as a bird   made of felt
because more   and more
of myself   is now
marked by   a realising
past   not remembered
for a second   I was seized
by a rhythm   of obeisance
words   came to me
continuously   from a poem
you wrote   when I quoted
the phase   when the whole
began infinitely   to part

even if there is no time at all,

composition comes—

it never fails any one

in the afterwards
of thought,

when the force
of the subsequent

inevitably queries all
the continuous points

that have preceded,
brevity—now and then—

does not always have
to be brief

being being being being being being
being being being being being being being
being   being   being   being   being
being   being   being   being
and   and   and   and   and
and   and   and
and and and
and   and
and
and
and and
and and and
and   and   and
and   and   and   and   and
time   time   time   time
time   time   time   time   time
time time time time time time time
time   time   time   time   time   time

before me

time perches on
    the initial design
        now susceptible

to some other,
    troublesome sight—

a naturally,   almost universally
        repeating view
  of
    nothing,   of

its true extent,

    a concluding and a beginning

        again and again
    that even it
  itself
cannot
  precisely remember

at once   the mind — excited by the melancholy of choice —   throws us   on a necessary course   of contrast   —   of sorrow and consideration   of lists and purposes   of supremeness and impression   of doubt and totality   of quality and distribution of soul and circumstance   of trouble and phenomena   of elucidation and intention of aid and advantage   of instance and application   of lover and self-torture of mistress and subservience   of interest and properties   of reason and melancholy of point and variation   of name and beginning   of Beauty and attainment   of intellect and occasion   of fancy and difficulty   of door and answer   of word and assumption   of never and tone   of either and also   of contrast and contrast

Back in the sacred province of influences, where the deceased invariably spring from the living,

     the poem was in the beak of the Raven again.

                             Even long after
                                I had taken the fifth,

          it was still
              (just nearly)

                  beginning to take form—

Notes on the Text

the transmission of (other subsurface agents may be considered necessary for underground Control (page 16)

This poem was specially written for a 2011 reading at the Exit Art gallery in New York City in conjunction with the exhibition "Fracking: Art and Activism Against the Drill." "Fracking," short for "hydraulic fracturing," is a technique of drilling for natural gas that entails injecting vast quantities of water into the earth along with sand and a mixture of proprietary (and toxic) chemicals in order to fracture the underground shale and release the gas. The title and epigraph of this poem were derived from words extracted from Sect. 322 and Sec. 323 of the ENERGY POLICY ACT OF 2005. The text was printed, cut up, then soaked in water along with a "proprietary" blend of chemicals that I found in my medicine cabinet; words were then chosen according to "proprietary" principals of selection. The body of the poem draws on words only found in Christopher Bateman's article "A Colossal Fracking Mess" which appeared in *Vanity Fair* (June 21, 2010) along with a video and photographs by Jacques del Conte.

Menu in Chinglish (page 19)

This poem was inspired by the phrase "monolithic tree mushroom stem squid" which occurs in the *New York Times* article "Shanghai Is Trying to Untangle the Mangled English of Chinglish" (May 2, 2010).

(Be)labored Posterities (page 20)

I am a revolutionary so that my son can be a farmer and his son can be a poet. Qtd. in <http://occupywallst.org/forum/i-am-a-revolutionary-so-my-son-can-be-a-farmer-so-/>. This phrase, which is often attributed to Thomas Jefferson, appears to be a vernacular paraphrase and condensation of a passage John Adams wrote to Abigail in 1780: "I must study politics and war that my sons may have liberty to study mathematics and philosophy. My sons ought to study mathematics and philosophy, geography, natural history, naval architecture, navigation, commerce, and agriculture, in order to give their children a right to study painting, poetry, music, architecture, statuary, tapestry, and porcelain."

Fruits and Flowers and Animals and Seas and Lands Do Open (page 41)

This sequence grew out of a 2013 National Poetry Month initiative sponsored by the *Found Poetry Review*. Entitled "Pulitzer Remix," this online and ephemeral project entailed eighty-five poets posting new poems every day based on the language of the eighty-five books which have won the Pulitzer Prize in fiction. After volunteering to participate, I was assigned Booth Tarkington's *Alice Adams* (1921), a comedic novel of manners set in the Midwest. All of the words in this thirty-part long poem, with no exception, were derived from Tarkington's text, and all of the thirty sections of this poem were composed daily throughout the thirty days of April. This is, in essence, a document of my life as I lived it in April 2013 through the obsessive reading, rereading, and remixing of a single book, an experiment of what happens when a life makes poetry, at least the writing of it, a priority for thirty continuous days despite all else.

The Philosophy of Decomposition / Recomposition as Explanation: A Poe and Stein Mash-Up (page 91)

All the words and marks of punctuation from "The Philosophy of Decomposition" are derived from the following two source texts. There was one minor (and hopefully forgivable) exception. On several occasions, I plundered the vocabulary of this note, which accompanied the Poe essay: "The quotations from 'The Raven' are centered here for the convenience of the reader. As the columns are rather narrow, these quotations are not centered, or even indented, in the original, but presumably would have been had space allowed."

Poe, Edgar Allan. "The Philosophy of Composition." *Graham's Magazine* 28.4 (1846): 163–167. The Edgar Allan Poe Society of Baltimore. Web. 10 May 2010. <http://www.eapoe.org/works/essays/philcomp.htm>.

Stein, Gertrude. "Composition as Explanation." *A Stein Reader.* Ed. Ulla Dydo. Evanston: Northwestern University Press, 1993, 493–503. Print.

Acknowledgments

Thanks to the editors of the following magazines for first publishing versions of these poems: *Action, Yes; eccolinguistics; Interim; jubilat; Marsh Hawk Review; Modern Language Studies; New American Writing; Otoliths; The Recluse;* and *So and So Magazine.*

An excerpt of "The Philosophy of Decomposition" appeared in *The &Now Awards 2: The Best Innovative Writing* (Lake Forest College Press, 2013).

Some of these poems also appeared in the following chapbooks: *The Philosophy of Decomposition/Re-composition as Explanation: A Poe and Stein Mash-Up* (Delete Press, 2011), *Words on Edge* (Plan B Press, 2012), and *Fruits and Flowers and Animals and Seas and Lands Do Open* (Burnside Review Press, 2015).

About the Author

Michael Leong is the author of several books, most recently *Cutting Time with a Knife*, also from Black Square, and the electronic collection *Who Unfolded My Origami Brain?*, from Fence Digital. His poetry has been anthologized in *THE &NOW AWARDS 2: The Best Innovative Writing* and *Best American Experimental Writing 2018*. A recipient of a Literature Translation Fellowship from the National Endowment for the Arts, he is Assistant Professor of English at the University at Albany, SUNY, where he teaches creative writing and literary study.